9-10

Turkey Hunting

Sloan MacRae

PowerKiDS press

New York

Published in 2011 by The Rosen Publishing Group, Inc.
29 East 21st Street, New York, NY 10010

First Edition

Editor: Amelie von Zumbusch
Book Design: Greg Tucker
Photo Researcher: Julio Gil

Photo Credits: Cover, pp. 6, 7, 8, 9, 10, 11, 12, 14–15, 16, 17, 18, 19, 20, 21, 22 (top), 25, 26–27, 29 Shutterstock.com; p. 4 Buyenlarge/Getty Images; p. 5 © www.iStockphoto.com/David Clumpner; p. 13 Niall Benvie/Getty Images; pp. 22 (bottom), 23, 28 © www.iStockphoto.com/Jon Huelskamp; p. 24 © www.iStockphoto.com/Stacey Newman.

Library of Congress Cataloging-in-Publication Data

MacRae, Sloan.
  Turkey hunting / Sloan MacRae. — 1st ed.
    p. cm. — (Open season)
  Includes index.
  ISBN 978-1-4488-0709-3 (library binding) — ISBN 978-1-4488-1379-7 (pbk.) — ISBN 978-1-4488-1380-3 (6-pack)
  1. Turkey hunting—Juvenile literature. I. Title.
  SK325.T8M233 2011
  799.2'4645—dc22
                                        2010009528

Manufactured in the United States of America

CPSIA Compliance Information: Batch #WS10PK: For Further Information contact Rosen Publishing, New York, New York at 1-800-237-9932

Contents

Big Birds

People call baseball the national **pastime**, but a case can definitely be made for turkey hunting as the national pastime, too. The wild turkey is native to North America. Native Americans hunted turkeys for thousands of years.

Native Americans used many parts of the turkeys they hunted. This Oglala man is wearing a headdress made with turkey feathers.

Hunting Facts

Wild turkeys often weigh more than 20 pounds (9 kg). That is a big bird!

This turkey hunter proudly shows off the bird he has just shot. There are several million turkey hunters in the United States today.

The turkey was **sacred** to some native peoples. Native Americans often wore turkey feathers in their headdresses. European settlers saw turkeys for the first time when they arrived in the New World.

The statesman Benjamin Franklin once suggested that the turkey would make a better national bird of the United States than the bald eagle. Franklin argued that the eagle was cowardly and lazy, while the turkey was very brave and never backed down from a fight.

Today, turkeys are still important in the United States. Millions of Americans celebrate Thanksgiving every year by eating turkey. Most of us eat turkeys that come from farms. These birds have been fattened up, most often on corn.

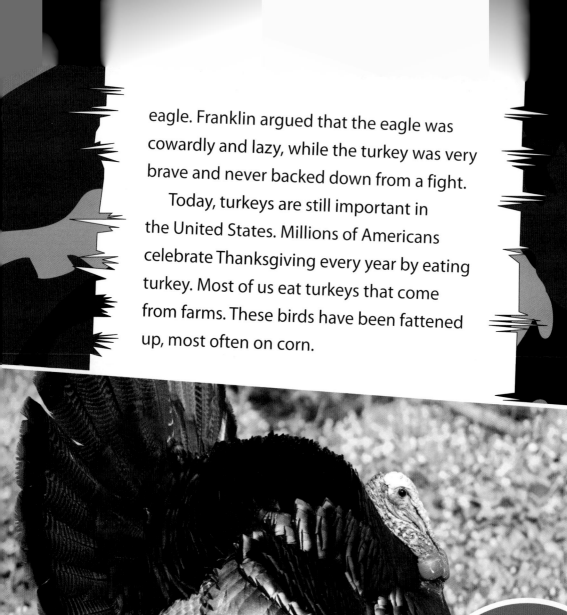

Wild turkeys, such as the bird here, live in many places, including woods, grasslands, swamps, and chaparral.

These domestic turkeys are being raised on a farm. Unlike wild turkeys, domestic turkeys are often white.

Wild turkeys do not taste quite like **domestic** ones. Turkeys are naturally **omnivores**. This means they do not eat only plants. They also hunt for insects. Wild turkeys eat anything they can find.

Turkey hunters prefer the meat of wild turkeys to the **poultry** sold in grocery stores. They also enjoy the challenge presented by hunting these big birds. That makes them taste even better.

Spring and Fall Gobblers

Many animals are hunted in the cold of fall and winter, but turkey hunters also hunt in the warmer spring months. Most states have spring gobbler seasons. Gobblers are male turkeys. They are much larger and provide more meat than the females, or hens.

Turkey hunting is usually permitted in the fall as well. Some **purists** consider fall turkey hunting to be better

This wild turkey is a hen. It is sometimes against the law to shoot hens. Learn your state's laws before you go turkey hunting!

sport because it is more challenging. It is harder to get gobblers to come to you in the autumn. Most states permit turkey hunting from dawn to dusk.

Wild turkeys live in forested areas, but they avoid thick brush. Successful turkey hunters pick spots in the woods that offer clear fields of vision for shooting.

Gobblers, such as the one shown here, are larger and more colorful than females are. Male turkeys are also sometimes known as toms.

Unlike some baby birds, wild turkey chicks, such as this one, are able to follow their mothers around and find food very soon after they hatch.

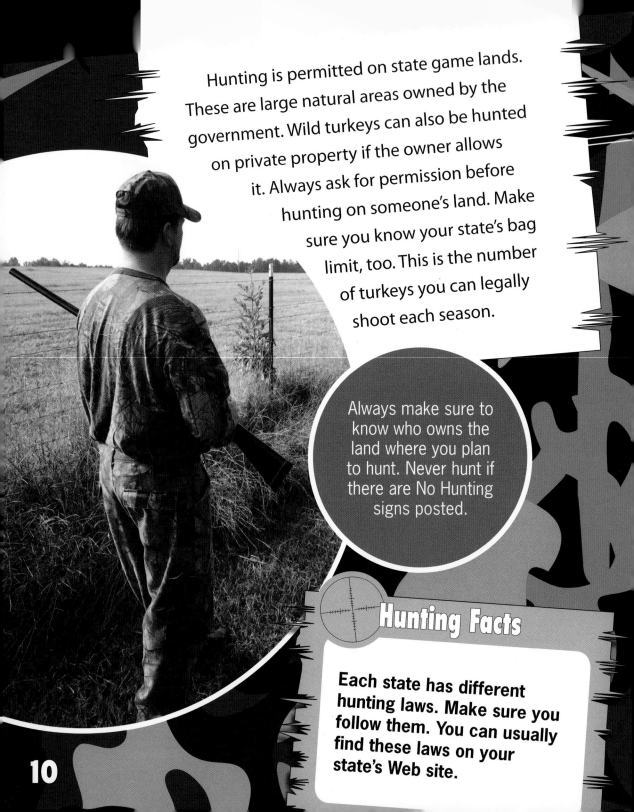

Hunting is permitted on state game lands. These are large natural areas owned by the government. Wild turkeys can also be hunted on private property if the owner allows it. Always ask for permission before hunting on someone's land. Make sure you know your state's bag limit, too. This is the number of turkeys you can legally shoot each season.

Always make sure to know who owns the land where you plan to hunt. Never hunt if there are No Hunting signs posted.

Hunting Facts

Each state has different hunting laws. Make sure you follow them. You can usually find these laws on your state's Web site.

Camouflage

You have probably seen hunters wearing bright orange. This protects them from being mistaken for animals by other hunters. Unfortunately, turkeys can see colors. They will avoid a hunter decked out in orange. Therefore, hunters wear **camouflage** when turkey hunting. Camouflage patterns help hunters blend in with the woods. It is a good idea to wear camouflage gloves to hide the color of your hands and a camouflage mask or camouflage makeup for your face.

This man's jacket, hat, and gloves have a camouflage pattern that makes him harder to see.

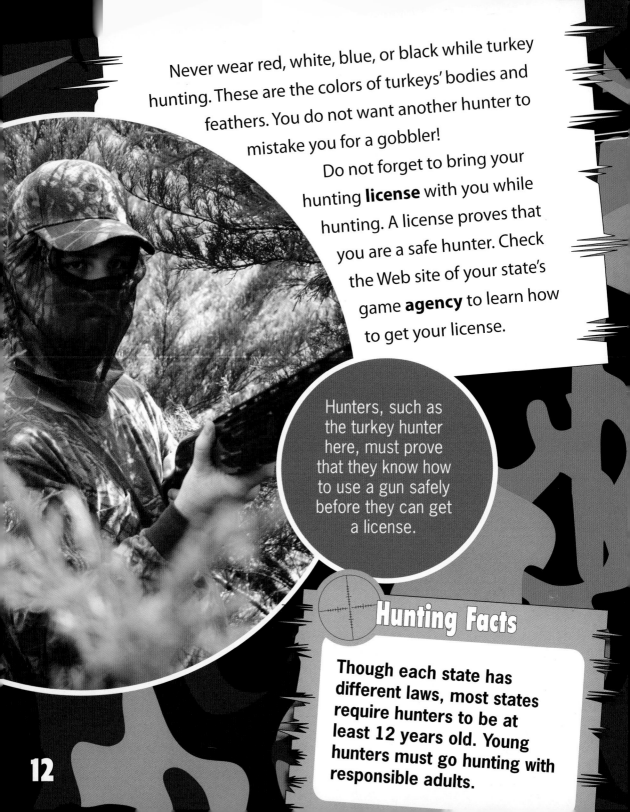

Never wear red, white, blue, or black while turkey hunting. These are the colors of turkeys' bodies and feathers. You do not want another hunter to mistake you for a gobbler!

Do not forget to bring your hunting **license** with you while hunting. A license proves that you are a safe hunter. Check the Web site of your state's game **agency** to learn how to get your license.

Hunters, such as the turkey hunter here, must prove that they know how to use a gun safely before they can get a license.

Hunting Facts

Though each state has different laws, most states require hunters to be at least 12 years old. Young hunters must go hunting with responsible adults.

Shotguns

The best firearm for hunting turkeys is the shotgun. At first glance, shotguns might appear similar to rifles, but they are very different. A rifle shoots a single bullet. A shotgun shoots a shell. The shells used in turkey hunting are tightly packed with small pellets, called shot. The shot explodes out of the barrel and scatters in a small area.

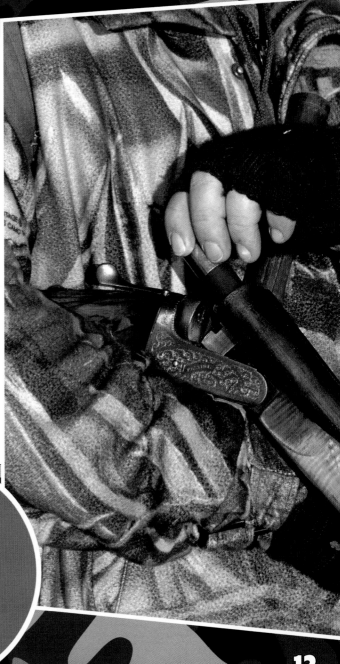

Here, you can see a hunter loading, or putting a shell into, a shotgun. Different kinds of shotguns are loaded in different ways.

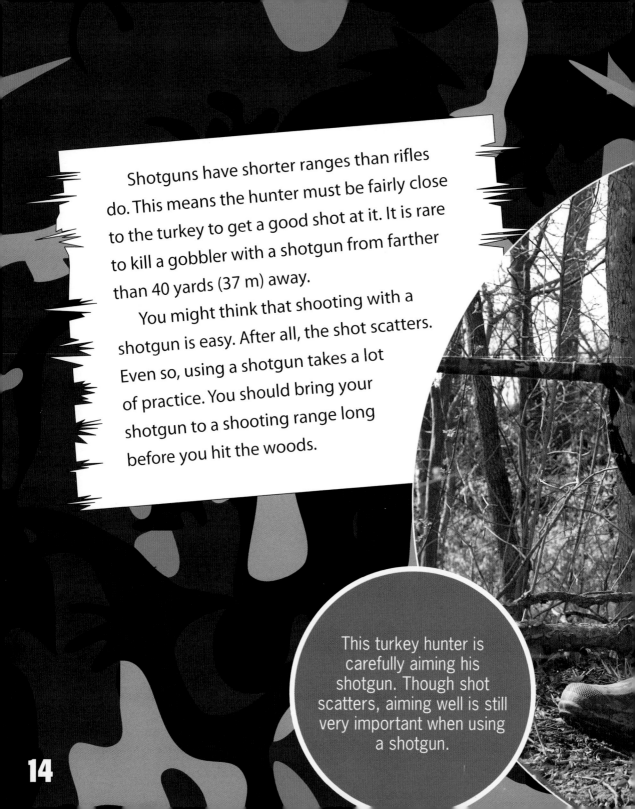

Shotguns have shorter ranges than rifles do. This means the hunter must be fairly close to the turkey to get a good shot at it. It is rare to kill a gobbler with a shotgun from farther than 40 yards (37 m) away.

You might think that shooting with a shotgun is easy. After all, the shot scatters. Even so, using a shotgun takes a lot of practice. You should bring your shotgun to a shooting range long before you hit the woods.

This turkey hunter is carefully aiming his shotgun. Though shot scatters, aiming well is still very important when using a shotgun.

Sporting clubs often have shooting ranges where hunters can bring their firearms. Practice will help you shoot in tight patterns. In other words, you will be more

Hunting Facts

Be careful when using a shotgun! Always keep your shotgun's safety on until you are ready to fire. Never point the gun at yourself or another person.

likely to hit your **targets**. Shooting at the range will also help you learn to estimate, or guess, distances. While you are there, you might even try shooting at a target that features a picture of a turkey!

This hunter is practicing her shooting at a shooting range. You can see a group of red shotgun shells lined up in front of the hunter.

Some turkey hunters who like to be challenged prefer to hunt with bows. Humans have used bows for several thousand years. Modern compound bows are far more advanced than the ones our **ancestors** used, but the basic way they work is still the same.

Bowstrings send arrows to the target, and archers must have very good aim in order to hit it. It is important

This turkey hunter is using a compound bow. The pulleys on a compound bow give the arrows that the bow shoots greater force.

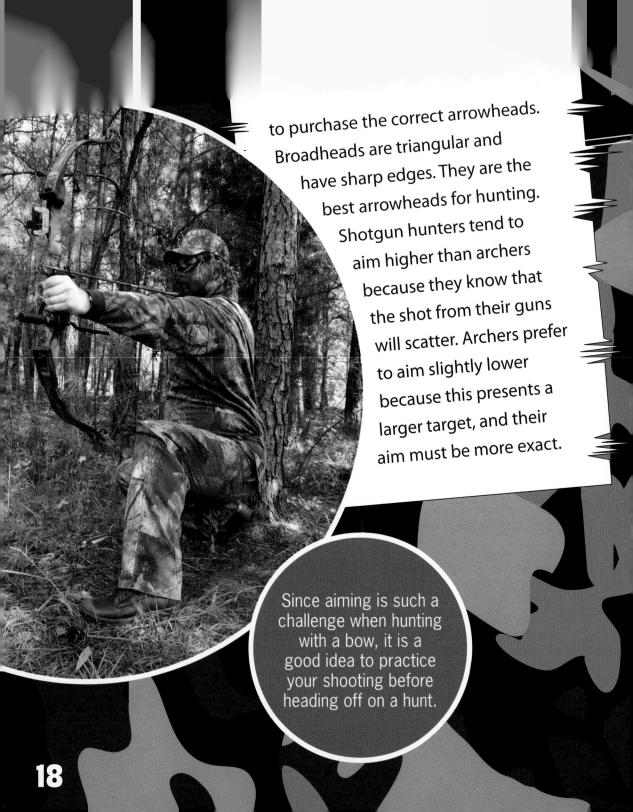

to purchase the correct arrowheads. Broadheads are triangular and have sharp edges. They are the best arrowheads for hunting. Shotgun hunters tend to aim higher than archers because they know that the shot from their guns will scatter. Archers prefer to aim slightly lower because this presents a larger target, and their aim must be more exact.

Since aiming is such a challenge when hunting with a bow, it is a good idea to practice your shooting before heading off on a hunt.

It is a good idea to scout the area in which you plan to hunt before the season begins. You can learn to follow tracks, and you might even see some turkeys. You can discover where they travel and find the best spots for shooting them. Getting to know the area will also prevent you from getting lost.

Even if you do it several months before the hunting season starts, scouting the area where you plan to hunt, as this girl is doing, is helpful.

Turkey hunters use different methods from those used by the hunters of other animals. For example, some animals are best hunted by stalking them. This is a very bad idea when hunting gobblers. It is almost impossible to sneak up on one. It is also unsafe. Remember, turkey hunters do not wear orange. What you think is a turkey might actually be another turkey hunter!

Though it is unwise to stalk gobblers, it is a good idea to learn the types of places they can be found. This helps you pick a good hunting spot.

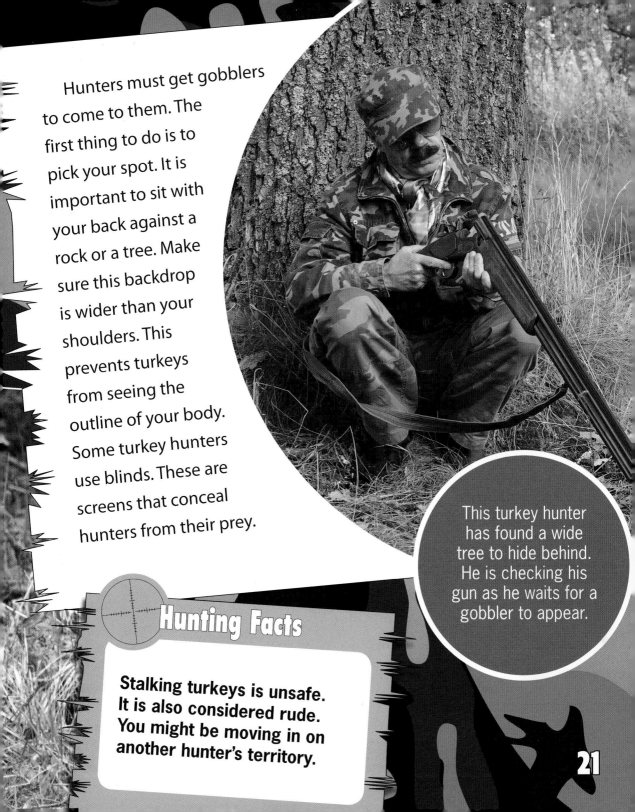

Hunters must get gobblers to come to them. The first thing to do is to pick your spot. It is important to sit with your back against a rock or a tree. Make sure this backdrop is wider than your shoulders. This prevents turkeys from seeing the outline of your body. Some turkey hunters use blinds. These are screens that conceal hunters from their prey.

This turkey hunter has found a wide tree to hide behind. He is checking his gun as he waits for a gobbler to appear.

Hunting Facts

Stalking turkeys is unsafe. It is also considered rude. You might be moving in on another hunter's territory.

Other tricks include using decoys and calls. Decoys are basically fake turkeys. They can draw real birds to you. Calls are tools used to imitate the sounds made by turkeys. Be careful. Decoys and calls can also fool hunters. Always cover a decoy when you carry it. Never make calls if you think another hunter is nearby. Instead, greet the hunter in a clear voice.

If you look closely, you can see that these turkeys are actually decoys. The camouflage tent behind them is a blind.

There are several kinds of turkey calls. This is a slate call. The round part is the slate, and the black piece on top is the striker.

Thanksgiving Dinner in April?

How do you turn your bird into a delicious meal? The first thing you must do is field dress your gobbler. Field dressing, or cleaning, prevents the meat from spoiling. It is always smart to bring a sharp knife, garbage bags, and plastic gloves on your hunt. You do not have to remove

This hunter is carrying home a turkey that he has shot. Turkeys are heavy, so make sure you have a plan for getting yours home!

the feathers until you get the bird home. You must also fill out the tag from your hunting license and tag your bird. This reports the kill to your state's wildlife agency.

You can look online for creative recipes for cooking wild turkeys. You can also prepare the bird **traditionally** with stuffing and gravy. Do not be disappointed if your turkey does not taste exactly like Thanksgiving

This boy is biting into a turkey leg. Legs are dark meat. Wild turkeys have more dark meat than domestic turkeys do.

Wild turkeys, such as this gobbler, walk and run more often than domestic turkeys do. They also fly for short distances, which domestic turkeys cannot do.

dinner. Keep in mind that wild turkeys do not taste just like domestic ones.

Wild turkeys lead different lives. They are not fed by farmers. They must find their own food. They are far more active than their barnyard cousins. This gives them a more **intense** flavor.

Protecting Turkeys

We are lucky that wild turkeys are still around. They nearly died out after many forests were cut down, and their **habitats** were destroyed. There were only 30,000 wild turkeys left in North America just 70 years ago.

Fortunately, organizations such as the National Wild Turkey Federation, or NWTF, have worked closely with federal, state, and local governments to bring the turkey back. The NWTF was created in 1973 because people

These wild turkeys are in Missouri. Attempts to reintroduce the turkey have been very successful. Today, wild turkeys are found in every U.S. state except for Alaska.

feared the wild turkey would vanish from the planet. Hundreds of hunters have joined this organization to help **conserve** and restore wild turkey habitats.

The hard work of groups like NWTF has paid off. Today, wild turkey populations are back in the millions. It is hard to believe these efforts were so successful over such a short time.

Hunters kill wild animals for sport, but it is important to remember that good hunters respect these animals. Hunters believe

Turkey hunters, such as this man, have played a big part in the comeback of the wild turkey.

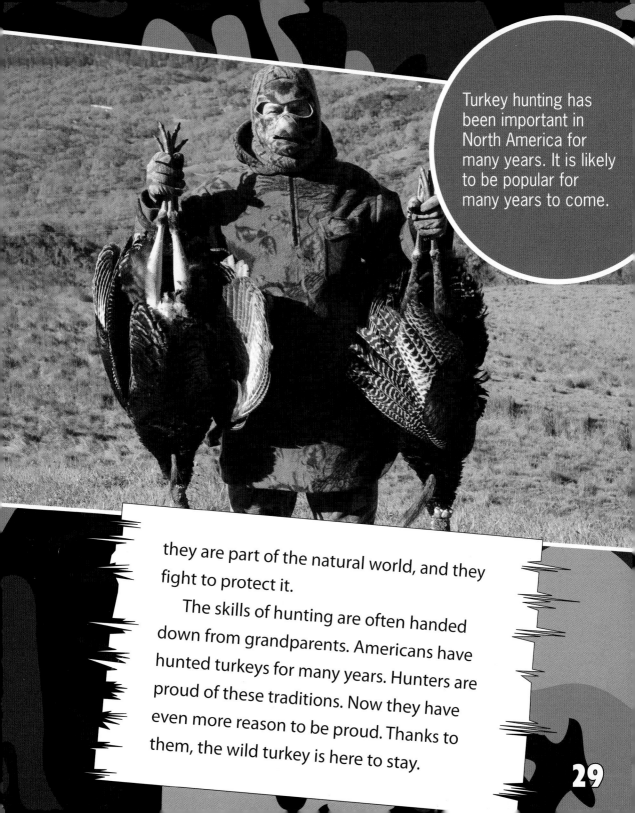

Turkey hunting has been important in North America for many years. It is likely to be popular for many years to come.

they are part of the natural world, and they fight to protect it.

The skills of hunting are often handed down from grandparents. Americans have hunted turkeys for many years. Hunters are proud of these traditions. Now they have even more reason to be proud. Thanks to them, the wild turkey is here to stay.

Happy Hunting

- ⊕ Never pull your trigger until you are absolutely sure of your target.

- ⊕ Study your state's hunting laws. Some states allow you to hunt hens in the fall. Do not shoot them if they are out of season, though.

- ⊕ Keep your ears open. Turkeys can make a lot of noise.

- ⊕ Always tag your kill. This helps your state keep track of turkey populations.

- ⊕ Try to get a map of the area if you plan to hunt on public lands.

- ⊕ Do not forget to bring extra shotgun shells. Most camouflage vests and jackets have deep pockets for shells.

- ⊕ Never carry a decoy without covering it first. You might use a sack or a camouflage blanket. You do not want another hunter shooting at your decoy while it is in your hands!

- ⊕ Do not forget to practice shooting before your hunt.

- ⊕ Clean and oil your shotgun before you put it away for the season.

- ⊕ Always be careful!

Glossary

agency (AY-jen-see) A special department of the government.

ancestors (AN-ses-terz) Relatives who lived long ago.

camouflage (KA-muh-flahj) A color or a pattern that matches the surroundings and helps hide something.

conserve (kun-SERV) To keep something from being wasted or used up.

domestic (duh-MES-tik) Having to do with animals made by people choosing which animals to breed together.

habitats (HA-buh-tats) The surroundings where animals or plants naturally live.

intense (in-TENTS) Very strong.

license (LY-suns) Official permission to do something.

omnivores (OM-nih-vorz) Animals that eat both plants and animals.

pastime (PAS-tym) An activity that makes time pass in an enjoyable way.

poultry (POHL-tree) Birds, such as chickens, raised for their meat or eggs.

purists (PYUHR-ists) People who stick to what they see as the correct way of doing things.

sacred (SAY-kred) Highly respected and considered very important.

targets (TAHR-gits) Things that are aimed at.

traditionally (truh-DIH-shuh-nuh-lee) In a way that has been passed down over time.

Index

A
agency, 12, 24
Americans, 6, 29

F
fall, 8, 30
feathers, 5, 12, 24
Franklin, Benjamin, 5–6

H
hunter(s), 7–9, 11–12,
    14–15, 17–18,
    20–22, 27–30

L
license, 12, 24

M
meat, 7–8, 23

N
Native Americans, 4–5
New World, 5
North America, 4, 26

O
omnivores, 7

P
pastime, 4
people(s), 4–5, 26
plants, 7
poultry, 7

purists, 8

S
stuffing, 24

T
target(s), 16–18, 30
turkey(s), 4–11, 13–14,
    16, 19–22, 24–27,
    29–30

U
United States, 5–6

W
winter, 8

Web Sites

Due to the changing nature of Internet links, PowerKids Press has developed an online list of Web sites related to the subject of this book. This site is updated regularly. Please use this link to access the list: www.powerkidslinks.com/os/th/

32